Contents

1

Part 1: Introduction

There are some stories that stay in peoples' collective consciousness forever - they don't seem to go away. Often they are stories with core morals and messages: things that concern humanity generation after generation. The novel that this guide will look at, *The Strange Case of Dr Jekyll and Mr Hyde*, is one of these stories. Written by Robert Louis Stevenson during the nineteenth century, the story is one of the most famous of the Victorian period and persists to the current day. The name of the novel, in fact, has almost become synonymous with the idea of someone having two sides - a good one and a bad one.

At the time of its publication, *The Strange Case of Dr Jekyll and Mr Hyde* became an instant classic. Shocking in its subject matter but also incredibly well written, the novel was read widely and, it is said, by everyone from those who didn't normally read fiction to the Queen herself. To this day there are new television and movie adaptations being made of the story - it's clearly one that has interested people for well over 100 years and shows no signs of going out of fashion soon. To date there have been over 123 film versions of the story, not to mention numerous stage and radio adaptations.

For a story that appears so familiar that many of us feel we know it before even opening the book, what are the reasons for reading Stevenson's original text? As you will see from this guide, there is a whole host of interesting themes, ideas and contexts at work underneath the seemingly straightforward reading of the novel. It explores in detail, in a way that was utterly shocking for its contemporary Victorian audience, the idea of the human being comprising more than one personality, that there is both good and evil lurking in men and that, sometimes, we are unable to control these competing qualities.

As well as addressing a number of interpretations of the events in the story, contextual features and the setting of the novel, in this guide I will aim to give you everything you need to be able to discuss the language, structure and characters of *The Strange Case of Dr Jekyll and Mr Hyde*. I hope you find it useful!

Part 2: Chapter Summaries

Chapter 1 – The story of the door

In this, the opening chapter of the story, we are introduced to the character of Mr Utterson. Mr Utterson is a lawyer who, it is pointed out, is very reliable. We are told about how he is very understanding of other people and is very slow to judge them. We also learn that he is loyal and very careful about who he becomes friends with. Mr Utterson goes out walking every Sunday with a cousin of his, a Mr Richard Enfield, and it is on one of these walks that they happen to wander down a side-street in a busy area of London. It is a very attractive area where all the residents are quite wealthy and successful. This is disturbed by a building, which is described as "sinister". It is described as being neglected and, on the outside, its doorways frequented by tramps and gangs of children.

Upon seeing this building, Enfield tells Utterson of a story about how, one night at three in the morning, he was walking home and he began to get an eerie sensation, a feeling that something was not right. All of a sudden, he saw two figures running towards each other from separate streets. One was a small man and the other a girl of around eight-years-old. When the two come upon each other, Enfield tells us, the man calmly tramples the young girl without even stopping.

He continues the story telling the reader and Utterson how a crowd gathered and how, for some "unnatural" reason, everyone took a severe dislike to this man. He appears to inspire a vicious hatred in the hearts and faces of all the people gathered around. Enfield repeatedly makes reference to how the man sneered and looked at everyone. Enfield and a doctor who stops by to help the girl both promise to ruin the man's reputation around town unless he pays £100 to the girl's family – a huge amount in those days.

The man agrees and goes in through the door of the building that Enfield had pointed out to Utterson on their walk. He returns with gold and a cheque to bring the sum to £100. Enfield doesn't trust the man – he recognizes the name that has been signed on the cheque although he won't mention it to Utterson. Not trusting the man, Enfield, the doctor and the child's father accompany him to the bank in the morning. It turns out the cheque is genuine, leading Enfield to believe that this man was blackmailing the man whose name is on the cheque, a man he believes to be of the highest reputation. As a result, he tells Utterson that he has come to refer to the house as "Black Mail House".

Utterson asks Enfield why he never investigated the matter to which Enfield replies – the more suspicious it looks, the less questions he asks. He mentions that he has observed the house on a number of occasions but has seen no one going in or out except for the man in his story. He also mentions that someone must be living there although it's difficult to tell where one house begins and another ends in that part of the street.

Finally, Utterson asks Enfield the name of the man from his story and Enfield tells him that it was a Mr Hyde. When asked to describe him, Enfield says that he's difficult to describe, that there is something "wrong" with his appearance, that he's "down-right detestable" but that he can't remember anything else.

Meanwhile, Utterson has managed to figure out who this other person is, the one whose name Enfield didn't want to mention, the man he believes is being blackmailed. Utterson asks Enfield to tell him if there were any untruths in his tale. Enfield, slightly offended, says there were not. They both agree not to speak of the matter ever again.

Chapter 2 – Search for Mr Hyde

Utterson returns to his home where he lives alone but is troubled by the matter Enfield has told him about. He's unable to enjoy his dinner or his after-dinner reading. Unable to settle, he goes to his safe and from it takes Dr Jekyll's will. We learn that although he has it in his possession, Utterson did not help Dr Jekyll prepare it. The will makes Mr Edward Hyde the beneficiary in the event of Dr Jekyll's death and, what's more, it also stipulates that should Dr Jekyll be missing for a period of at least three months, Mr Hyde should step into his shoes and inherit his wealth.

We learn that Utterson has long had misgivings over the will as he does not see it as normal and, following Enfield's story, he now believes that there is something much more sinister going on. He gets his coat and heads off to see a friend of both he and Dr Jekyll's: Dr Lanyon. Dr Lanyon is a man with a great reputation and Utterson decides that if anyone knows how to proceed it will be him.

When he arrives, the butler brings him straight in to see Dr Lanyon, despite the late hour. Dr Lanyon is a healthy man and appears at the prime of his life. There is a genuine friendship between the two men and we learn that they share this bond with Dr Jekyll also. However, Dr Lanyon and Dr Jekyll have had a disagreement of some sort and haven't spoken much in ten years. Lanyon admits that he keeps an eye on him and that their disagreement was on some point of science. Utterson asks him if he's ever heard of Hyde but Lanyon has not.

Utterson returns home but the matter still troubles him and all night he dreams of the story that Enfield told him, all the while being unable to see the man's face. It is from this moment that Utterson begins to hang around the side streets near the door in the hope of seeing Hyde.

Eventually all his snooping pays off and one night he sees who he thinks is Hyde. The area has gone very quiet and it becomes altogether frightening and eerie – similar to when Enfield was walking the streets before seeing Hyde himself. Even at a distance, Utterson has almost a physical reaction of revulsion to Mr Hyde. He approaches him and, addressing him by name, asks if he can be admitted to see Dr Jekyll. Hyde says Jekyll is not at home and asks how Utterson knew who he was. Utterson asks if he can see Hyde's face first and then he says that at least this way he will know him again in the future. Hyde asks him again how he knew him and he says from a friend's description. Hyde demands to know who and Utterson says they have Dr Jekyll in common and Hyde reacts angrily saying Jekyll would never have told Utterson anything about him and rushes into the house with a savage laugh.

Utterson is left standing outside the old door confused and with an increasingly bad opinion of Hyde. He begins to fear for his friend and calls around to the front of the house where Poole, the house servant, admits him to the hall and he sits by the fire. Poole returns shortly afterwards saying that Dr Jekyll has gone out. Utterson questions Poole about Hyde and he learns that all the staff have orders to obey Hyde and that he comes and goes as he pleases.

Utterson leaves the house and returns to his own with a heavy heart and full of worry for his friend. He reasons that Jekyll must have done something as a young man that Hyde is now blackmailing him about. He thinks for a while about the foolish things young men do and how they could easily come back to haunt older men. His biggest worry at this stage, however, is that if Hyde were to learn of the will then he may become impatient and something very bad indeed may happen to Dr Jekyll.

Chapter 3 – Dr. Jekyll was quite at ease

The story skips forward two weeks and a group is having dinner with Dr Jekyll at his home and Utterson is present. He makes sure to stay behind after everyone else has left and this, we are told, is nothing new. Utterson is well-liked and often his hosts would like to keep him late talking after others had departed.

It is during this conversation that Utterson reminds Jekyll of the will he has in his possession and how much he disapproves of it. Jekyll laughs him off and tries to change the subject but when Utterson mentions that he's been gathering information about Hyde, Jekyll grows pale and his face changes. He becomes sharp and tells Utterson that he is in a very strange and difficult situation and that it cannot be fixed by talking.

Utterson begs him to come clean promising to help him but Jekyll says that, though he appreciates the offer, it really isn't that serious a situation and promises Utterson that, should he wish, he could be rid of Hyde at a moment's notice.

Utterson takes his word on this but, before he leaves, Jekyll asks him to help Hyde when Jekyll himself is gone, as a personal favour. Utterson, while saying he can't pretend to like him, agrees to Jekyll's request.

Chapter 4 – The Carew murder case

Again, the story skips forward, this time to a year later. This chapter opens with the description of a terrible crime that, because the victim is a wealthy and high-status individual, shakes London to its core. The details of the case are related through the only eye-witness – a maid who was sitting at her window. We learn that there was a full moon and it was almost unnaturally bright. She sees a very handsome gentleman walking one way on the street and, towards him, a smaller man.

They come together and speak under her window. The handsome gentleman, who we are told had white hair, was very polite to the smaller man and it appears there was a request for directions. The maid watched the fine gentleman and admired him as he spoke before she laid eyes on the second man.

She recognized Hyde immediately as someone who had visited her master and someone she immediately disliked. She also notices that he holds a heavy cane in his hand. She reports that Hyde did not speak a word in return to the gentleman but in a rage, clubs him with the cane and proceeds to beat him to death.

She faints and, when she wakes, she calls the police, by which time Hyde has escaped. When the scene is investigated, they find some gold upon the victim and a letter that is addressed to Mr Utterson as well as half of the stick Hyde had been carrying.

The letter is taken to Utterson that morning and, once he opens it, he refuses to say another word until he has seen the body. Once he has, he identifies the victim as Sir Danvers Carew, a well-to-do gentleman. The police, realizing how much of a fuss will be created, ask Utterson if he can help in finding the culprit at which point Utterson is shown the half of the cane and recognizes it as Jekyll's. He takes the police to Hyde's address in Soho but he is not there. His landlady says that he had returned very late and left again. There was nothing strange in it, she said, because he had very peculiar habits. It is also at this stage that we learn how much Hyde stands to inherit should anything happen to Jekyll – a quarter of a million pounds. An incredible amount of money in the 19th century (let alone today).

When Utterson and the police look around his rooms, they notice that everything has been decorated and furnished in very good taste but also that it has recently been ransacked. Pockets in clothes are turned inside out and they find the charred remains of a cheque book in the fire as well as the other half of the stick behind a door. The policeman is delighted and says all they have to do is wait at the bank for him to try to make a withdrawal and they will have their man. The only difficulty is that so very few people have seen Hyde's face. In fact the only thing that people who have seen him agree on is the feeling of evil, disgust and revulsion that he inspires in them.

Chapter 5 – Incident of the letter

Utterson turns up at Jekyll's house in the afternoon and is shown in by Poole. He is in a part of the house that he's not been in before – a part that used to be an anatomical lecture hall where students would watch surgeons perform autopsies and learn from the practice. For Jekyll, we learn he was more interested in chemicals, so much of the area is used as storage and its emptiness gives Utterson an eerie feeling.

They pass through this area up to Jekyll's chambers and Poole delivers him to where Jekyll is sitting by the fire and a change has come over him. He looks sickly and his voice has changed from the handsome, entertaining man in earlier chapters. Utterson asks if Jekyll has heard of Carew's murder and, when he says he has, Utterson asks if he's hiding the man in his house. Jekyll says he is not and that no more will ever be heard from Hyde. Utterson mistrusts his friend as he observes that something has changed in him but he goes along with it.

Jekyll then confides in him that he has received a letter and only trusts Utterson with it. It is from Hyde and confirms that he has escaped and will not be returning. This soothes Utterson's worries and he agrees to keep the letter until they have decided what to do with it.

Utterson also says that he believes Hyde was behind the stipulation in Jekyll's will and that Jekyll had a lucky escape – that Hyde probably meant to murder him. On his way out, Utterson checks with Poole, the servant, if a letter had been delivered that day and when Poole says no, he is again suspicious and the mystery deepens. At this point we also learn that Sir Danvers Carew, the murder victim, was in fact a member of parliament – a very high-profile individual.

Later that evening with Mr Guest, his head clerk and a student of handwriting, Utterson attempts to figure out the letter that Jekyll has given him. Guest is familiar with Jekyll's handwriting as someone who would write to Utterson often through business and pleasure. Utterson gives him Hyde's letter to examine and just then another servant arrives with an invitation to dinner from no other than Jekyll. Guest examines both and declares that it is the same handwriting only with an attempted disguise. Utterson tells Guest not to speak of it and then he locks the letter away with a bad feeling.

Chapter 6 – Incident of Dr. Lanyon

As time goes on, rewards are offered for the capture of Sir Danvers Carew's murderer but he is not to be found. In this time also, Utterson grows calmer about the situation, believing Hyde to be gone for good and Jekyll begins to return to his old self – entertaining friends at his home and visiting others. We are told that physically, he even begins to look like he did in recent years – healthy and at peace.

This lasted two months before Jekyll again stops seeing his friends and giving Poole instruction to send visitors away. Utterson, again, decides to visit their mutual friend Dr Lanyon. Here he finds Lanyon very ill – physically, the illness is very visible on him. He is pale, gaunt, balder and his eyes have taken on a frightened manner. Lanyon tells Utterson that he has had a shock and he does not think he will recover. He believes he will die in a matter of weeks. Utterson remarks that Jekyll is ill too and this brings a change in Lanyon who says that he will not hear mention of that man anymore and that he is done with him. Lanyon asks that if he stays, Utterson is to talk of anything else but Jekyll because he can't bear it.

After arriving home, Utterson writes a letter to Jekyll complaining about being kept out of his house and asking about the fall-out with Dr Lanyon. Jekyll replies that he agrees that he and Lanyon should never meet again and tells Utterson that he intends to live a life of seclusion, seeing no one, until he dies. He says that this "darkness", he has brought on himself and begs Utterson to respect his wishes. Within two weeks, Lanyon has died and the night after the funeral he goes into his office, locks the door and takes out a letter written to Utterson by Lanyon but only to be opened after his death. Within that envelope, there is another that is marked "not to be opened till the death or disappeareance of Dr Henry Jekyll". Respecting his friend's wishes, Utterson returns the letter to his safe. He desires to speak with Jekyll but when he arrives, he is denied entry and instead, speaks with Poole at the doorway. He learns from Poole that the doctor confines himself to his chambers all day and night. It didn't appear that he slept and he believes something is troubling his master.

Chapter 7 – Incident at the window

Some time later, on one of their Sunday walks, Utterson and his cousin Enfield happen to walk past the door that they had stopped in front of earlier in the novel. Utterson tells Enfield that he once saw the man Hyde that Enfield had seen trample the young girl and he also tells him that he shared his feelings of revulsion and disgust upon seeing him.

Utterson and Enfield step into the courtyard of Jekyll's home as Utterson admits that he is worried for his old friend and wants to have a look around. At one of the windows, looking miserable and sick, they see Dr Jekyll.

Utterson calls up that he is looking better but Jekyll replies that he is not and that he believes he will die soon. Suddenly, mid-conversation, Jekyll's face begins to change and a look of utter terror and despair comes over him before he quickly pulls down the blind.

The two men leave quickly and, when they are some distance away, they look at each other's faces which are full of horror and they walk on in silence.

Chapter 8 – The last night

It is evening and Utterson is sitting by his fire when there is a visit from Poole who is clearly distressed. Poole tells him that he has been afraid for about a week and something is happening with Dr Jekyll and he doesn't like it. He admits to Utterson that he thinks Jekyll has been murdered. Utterson gets his coat and his hat immediately and agrees to follow Poole to Jekyll's house.

When they arrive at the house, the housemaid is whimpering and hysterical and Utterson admonishes her and the other staff for all being in the hallway saying Jekyll would not like it.

Poole takes Utterson around the back and begs him to be as quiet as possible as he wants him to hear and not be heard. They arrive at Jekyll's chamber door and Poole tells him that Mr Utterson is here to see him. A voice comes from behind the door saying he cannot see him and Poole and Utterson return to the kitchen. Here, Poole says that he has been working for Jekyll for twenty years and he knows for definite that that is not his master's voice. He believes he has been murdered because a few days previous they heard a lot of shouting and crying out.

Utterson cannot understand why, if someone has murdered Jekyll, they would stay at the scene all this time. Poole tried to explain it by saying that whatever is behind the door has been calling out for a type of medicine that Jekyll used to keep but had been unable to get a hold of recently. He had become frantic to get it, sending out to chemists all over London but not finding any that was pure enough. Now the person who has replaced Jekyll, Poole says, has been doing the same, giving orders to the staff to try this chemist and that for the powder.

Poole then tells Utterson that he has seen the man who is behind the door. He says that he saw him digging through crates in the storage area and says that, if it was his master, he must have been wearing a mask.

Utterson believes he has an answer and suggests that maybe Jekyll has one of those diseases that transform and disfigure the sufferer's face and that is why he is looking for medicine – to help him go back to normal. Poole rejects this completely arguing that what he saw was not his master and they both come to the conclusion that there is nothing left to do but break the door down and find out the truth.

They get the help of another servant, Bradshaw, to stand guard with a pair of sticks while Poole takes an axe and Utterson a poker. Poole and Utterson stand outside the door listening and decide that what they hear is not Jekyll's footsteps. Before they break the door down, Utterson calls out his final warning and when the voice responds, Utterson is finally convinced that it is Hyde in the room. They knock through the door and inside find the figure of Hyde on the carpet twictiching and wearing clothes that are much too big for him. They notice a vial in his hand and Utterson knows that Hyde has taken a substance and killed himself.

They look around the rest of the apartment for the body of Jekyll but are unable to find it. They are entirely confused. Utterson then finds a book that Jekyll had much admired and spoken highly of but now there were terrible things written about it in the margins of the book in Jekyll's own handwriting. This unsettles Utterson greatly and finally, after more searching, they find a letter on a table addressed to Utterson. He opens it and a few more letters fall out. The first is a will, similar to the previous one with one exception. Instead of leaving everything to Hyde, Jekyll was leaving everything to Utterson. The next note is dated with that day's date and addressed to Utterson.

In it, Jekyll says that he has disappeared and that he should go and read the letter Dr Lanyon gave to him. Utterson takes the third letter and then goes home to read that and the one that Lanyon gave him.

Chapter 9 – Dr. Lanyon's narrative

This chapter is Lanyon's letter to Utterson and, as such, Lanyon is the narrator. He tells us that four days ago he received a letter from Jekyll. This is surprising as they had fallen out previously and were not in touch. He then includes the content of the letter, which begs him for help and asks him, at once, to come to his house where Poole will be waiting with a locksmith to break in to his chambers. Lanyon is to go in alone to a specific drawer and take a vial, some powders and a book. He is to then take these items back to his house and wait until midnight when a man, who will present himself as Jekyll, will call for them. He is to hand them over and, through this, will save Jekyll's life.

Lanyon, after reading, decides that Jekyll must be insane but still feels duty-bound to comply. He goes to the house and does everything asked of him. Afterwards, looking at the pocket book, he sees a series of dates going over a number of years but that the dates ended "quite abruptly" around a year ago and there is a single word written at that point: "double".

Again, Lanyon, decides to follow Jekyll's wishes but loads an old revolver in case the caller isn't as trustworthy as his old friend. At midnight, a man calls and Lanyon is immediately hit by how much he dislikes him. He comments that he looked disfigured and made his skin crawl but couldn't put his finger on exactly why. The man is desperate for the contents of the drawer and is quite abrupt with Lanyon. He asks for a glass and mixes some of the powders there in the room with Lanyon.

He then says to Lanyon that, if he wants, he can get an explanation and see what is about to happen or, if he wants, the man can leave with the contents and Lanyon will be none the wiser. Lanyon says he wants to see and the man reminds him that what he is about to see is to remain entirely private. The man drinks the potion and turns into Dr Henry Jekyll. Lanyon is horrified. He says that his life has been shaken to its roots and he is unsure if he believes what he saw or not.

Lanyon signs off the letter by saying that, according to Jekyll, the man who called at midnight to his house was Mr Hyde, the murderer of Sir Carew.

Chapter 10 – Henry Jekyll's full statement of the case

This chapter consists of Henry Jekyll's letter to Utterson explaining the events of the novel. Again, our narrator changes, this time to Jekyll.

He begins by telling us about his background – heir to a large fortune, with a desire to work and to be thought well of by his friends and acquaintances. It is because of this, he says, that he began to hide his pleasures and regard them with a morbid sense of shame. He discusses then the "dual nature" of men where we have to balance the good and bad sides of our characters and how people restrain themselves from certain things in the name of decency or being a good person. He admits that his scientific work was leading him in the direction of the mystical and he comes to discover that man is not just one person, but two. He suggests that it may turn out, after further discoveries, that man is more than two, even a collection of different personalities and states. Jekyll's work focuses on the idea of the moral split in man, the division between good and bad. He admits that he was in touch with both sides of his character even before his interest in the scientific side of it developed. His experiments, he says, showed him that certain chemicals could draw back the barrier between these two sides of man but that, as his letter will show, his discoveries were incomplete. He waited quite a while before putting his potion to the test as he was quite worried that it might kill him but eventually he does and he is full of pain, sickness and a "horror of the spirit" before they all went away and he was left as Mr Hyde. He felt younger, happier and freer – knowing that he could do whatever he pleased. He says he knew immediately that he was wicked but he was happy to embrace it. At this stage he realized that he had become smaller. When he looked in the mirror, he could see that evil was imprinted on Hyde's face and body. Jekyll realized that anyone who saw Hyde would react badly to him because, all people are a mix of good and evil but Hyde was all evil and people recognized it in him. Worried about what might happen if he was seen, he takes another potion and returns to the body of Jekyll.

That night, Jekyll says, he thought about the drug and knew that the drug itself was not good or evil, it simply brought about a change in the person who took it. The evil side of Jekyll, he says, began to take over. The powder tempted him and he fell into addiction. All he had to do was drink it and he could shake off the old, learned, kind professor and become the young, hell-raising Hyde.

He tells all the staff that they are to obey Mr Hyde and then he draws up the will leaving everything to Hyde in case of his death or disappearance. He indulges in many pleasures as Hyde – things he could never have done as Dr Jekyll – but pretty soon, Hyde's acts and deeds become more monstrous.

Some months later, Jekyll begins to lose control of the transformations and they begin to happen without his control. He wakes up one morning and he has yet to turn back to Jekyll. This terrifies him as his evil side is beginning to become more dominant.

He realizes he must choose between the two sides of himself. After much debate, he chooses Jekyll but, he admits, he still keeps Hyde's house in Soho and his clothes. After a few months, the desire to once again be Hyde proves too much and he takes another potion. This time however, having not used it for months, the potion unleashes a new anger in Hyde and it scares him. He decides that he will destroy all of Hydes things in Soho and revert to Jekyll for good. On his way, however, he runs into Carew and murders him. It is this act that puts Jekyll on the straight and narrow for another few months. He says to Utterson that he knows how much he tried to enjoy people's company and entertain people in the last few months. Unfortunately, although he doesn't take a potion, he finds himself one day transforming into Hyde. He arranges with Lanyon to get the powders from his chambers and then goes to Lanyon's house to get them.

After this, Jekyll realizes that he has to take the potion simply to remain as Jekyll, that Hyde has taken over completely and he transforms without warning at any hour of the day. Jekyll and Hyde are locked in a battle for power of the body they share and both detest and hate the other. It is in this despair that Jekyll spends his final weeks.

He keeps drinking potions but they have no effect and can't change him back. He is convinced that the first batch had some impurity in it that was the secret ingredient. Jekyll, at the end of the letter, just before returning to the body of Hyde, says that this is the hour of his death and he does not care what happens to Hyde afterwards.

Part 3: The author

Robert Louis Stevenson was a big star of the 19th century literary scene. Considered the "next big thing" by many other writers who were working at the same time as him, he was already very well known for the novel *Treasure Island* which was published in 1883 - three years before Jekyll and Hyde. *Treasure Island*, despite being a very good book entirely on its own merit, is considered first and foremost a children's book and it's to Stevenson's childhood we turn first to learn a bit more about *The Strange case of Dr Jekyll and Mr Hyde.*

Robert Louis Stevenson was born in Edinburgh, Scotland in December 1850. His father was a well-respected engineer specialising in the construction, design and maintenance of lighthouses (of which there were many on the Scottish coast - considered at this time to be one of the most dangerous areas for ships in the world). His mother was the daughter of a clergyman (a minister or a priest). Childhood was a time of difficulty for young Louis as he was a very sickly child. He was often so poorly that he missed long periods of school and his education was attended to by private tutors at home - sometimes he would receive his lessons while he was in bed.

Despite his long absences from school, Stevenson's father, Thomas, was confident that his son would become an engineer and follow in the family business. In fact, he was so confident of this that he didn't really see the point of his son going to school at all - he is reported to have told Louis that all school is good for is learning to sit on your bum! He believed that his son would learn all he had to about the family business by being an apprentice and going to work with his father when he was old enough.

As well as not believing very much in formal schooling for his son, Stevenson's father (and mother) used their wealth to secure every treatment and drug available at the time to treat their son's many illnesses and ailments (it's thought that he may have had tuberculosis which is a disease of the lungs that was very common in the Victorian period). Other than securing medication, Stevenson's parents - like many Victorian parents of the upper classes - left most of the actual day-to-day raising of their child to the live-in nanny. Her name was Alison Cunningham (known as 'Cummy') and it is to this woman that we can trace some of the ideas that appear decades later in *Jekyll and Hyde.*

Cummy was a deeply religious woman and a Calvinist: a very strict branch of Christianity. She influenced the young Stevenson greatly as she told him stories about the Covenanters (another, even stricter, branch of Christians in Scotland at the time) and the devil and what happened to people who lived an unchristian life. For Cummy, who thought that cards were of the devil and that people who broke the sabbath by playing games on a Sunday needed to be prayed for, this meant pretty much everyone. The particular stories that Stevenson would have heard are much to do with blood, sacrifice and hoping to be accepted into heaven after death. Stevenson himself spoke about the nightmares he used to have that left him "clinging to the horizontal bar of the bed with my knees and chin together, my soul shaken, my body convulsed with agony." Often the young Stevenson would dream of hell and admits himself that he was afraid to go to sleep some nights in case he died and wasn't accepted into heaven.

One of the stories that would have been very common at the time and was sure to have been known by Stevenson was that of a Scottish Covenanter, Major Thomas Weir. He was well-respected and looked up to by many as a most religious and devout man. He and his wife held services outdoors attracting many followers and his reputation grew and grew over the years. He was believed to be close to God because he dedicated his whole life to serving God. A great scandal arose, however, when towards the end of his life, he admitted that the whole thing was a sham, that he and his wife had been engaging in deeply unreligious activity (mostly sexual) and that he had lived a terrible life in private. When charged, he and his wife admitted to meeting the devil and making a pact with him. He was burnt at the stake and she was also sentenced to death. It's not hard to see some links between Major Weir's life and that of Stevenson's Dr Jekyll.

Victorian society was one where there was a great emphasis placed on how one behaved and the "proper" ways for men and women to act. It was important for men to be gentlemen and for women to be submissive, obedient and supportive. In this society, any mention of sex or sexuality was strictly forbidden. This is despite the fact that, quite obviously, sex was something that was happening. This divide, the idea that something which was occurring between men and women but could not be spoken about in a rational and normal way was something that Stevenson was very aware of and something which inhabits many of his stories but especially *Jekyll and Hyde*.

As Stevenson developed as a writer, he continually returned to this idea that a person is not simply one person, but has more than one personality or mindset that constantly battles with the other. We might see similarities today with the idea that there's an angel on one shoulder encouraging you to do the right thing while on the other there is a devil trying to lead you astray. Stevenson wrote letters to friends about his childhood spent ill in bed and, at times, suffering from dangerous fevers. It was at this time, he says, that he really became aware of another "person", another consciousness within him. He called the two "myself and the other fellow". The other fellow, he said, was careless, reckless and irrational. Again, the similarities between this and the novel he wrote are striking.

With the influence of his nanny, Cummy, and her visions of heaven and hell and his sharp recognition of the divide between the private person and the public person, we can begin to see *Jekyll and Hyde* as a very personal story for Stevenson which goes far beyond what most people thought of it when it was first published - that it was just a "shilling shocker". Stevenson was, in effect, living two lives. On one hand he was an up and coming engineer in a very successful family firm. This was his public face. In reality, however, he didn't derive any joy from engineering or the thought of working in the family business. He wanted to be a writer, something his father actively discouraged.

When he finally admitted that he didn't want to be an engineer, he was allowed to study law (which he never practised as he began to publish stories while he was studying). It was in this time that he began to associate with people his family would have considered of a very low order in Edinburgh's Old town (which you can read more about in the chapter on setting). Here it's believed that Stevenson even became friends with many prostitutes - another link to the repressive and secretive Victorian views on sexuality. These women were looked down upon as the lowest of the low despite often having many upper class "customers" who were also living this double life.

As we can see, Stevenson's upbringing and early life in the upper classes of Victorian British society forced him to both recognise and also to live this double life of being good and proper in your public life but battling inner desires and compulsions in your private life - something many people would argue still exists today. Most people would admit that they have thoughts or secrets that they would never share with anyone else and that it's important to behave in a certain way in public. *Jekyll and Hyde* takes much of Stevenson's personal life and adjusts it to ask the question - what if the dark side won out?

Part 4: The novel

As the "next big thing" of the Victorian literary scene, Robert Louis Stevenson seemed to have it all in front of him. He had fame and relative financial security following the success of *Treasure Island* and all he had to do was to write the great literary landmark that everyone expected of him rather than further exploit his considerable talents for money. Unfortunately for his friends and other contemporary writers, the next book was *Jekyll and Hyde.* The book was dismissed as a "shilling shocker", a cheap, quickly produced story of low quality that is consumed by the masses just for entertainment.

Although Stevenson didn't initially think much of his story (he was much more excited about the release of his book *Prince Otto: A Romance* which was published shortly after he finished the first draft of *Jekyll and Hyde*), he wasn't prepared to pass up the opportunity to make money. Ironically, the novel that made Stevenson's friends think that he had given up real literature has ended up being one of his enduring successes.

The novel itself was published in 1886 and, according to Stevenson, came to him in a dream whilst he was very ill and possibly close to death. He was confined to bed and had been given medication (one of the side effects was hallucinations) to ease his pain. During the night, his wife, Fanny, awoke to find him in the middle of a night terror. As she woke him, he is said to have scolded her as he was dreaming the story of *Jekyll and Hyde*. According to Stevenson, he dreamt two scenes from the story - the one of Dr Jekyll taking the powders that initiates the change into Hyde and the scene close to the beginning where Hyde tramples the young girl.

We have seen in the previous section the idea that Stevenson constantly thought about man's duality, that there is more than one side to each person. Here was a novel that discussed this idea in great detail. Stevenson himself said of the book that he had "long been trying to write a story on [the] subject, to find a body, a vehicle, for that strong sense of man's double being…" He certainly found that "vehicle" in *Jekyll and Hyde*.

Some of the key ideas in the novel, the nature of dreams revealing truths, of the subconscious and of the idea of drugs or powders releasing something within men, are all played out in Stevenson's own life. He believed quite strongly in the subconscious as revealing to him parts of his true self. He even said once that he couldn't take all the credit for his story as most of it came from his subconscious mind.

This idea of people having a dual nature or combining two personalities is played out over and over again in the novel but also in Stevenson's own life. This novel, which made him a superstar in Britain and America and lots of money, also cost him his reputation at the time as a "serious" writer. As we have seen in the previous chapter, Stevenson lived a sort of double life and his experiences of religion (through

Cummy and his parents) and of Victorian society made him somewhat critical of the hypocrisy and hidden side to people of the time.

We also mentioned earlier the Victorian's repressive attitude to sex and sexuality. It's interesting to note that many of the film or television versions of *Jekyll and Hyde* (which come many years later in the early 20th century) tend to depict Hyde as a sex-crazed monster, that women are unsafe around him, that his primary evil is lust and desire. This is interesting on a number of levels. Firstly, this isn't at all apparent in the novel on a surface level. It is however, suggested that after writing the first draft, his wife, Fanny, told him that it would never be published (due to decency laws) and that he had missed the opportunity to write an allegory, an extended metaphor about human behaviour. The subsequent redrafting, which removed many more obvious references to the previous sexual experiences of the characters involved, led to a much more subtle story where many things are hinted at but not exactly said.

In this case, is Stevenson saying that our dark sides, our "Mr Hydes", are primarily concerned with our sexuality and that repressing or covering them up so much is actually doing us harm? There is the suggestion that the novel is dealing with the idea of fighting our real desires or appetites in order to fit into Victorian society. The picture is of a London (or Edinburgh) in the 1800s full of men who, to the outside world look respectable and trustworthy, but underneath are fighting against their own terrible desires. This would have been incredibly shocking at the time it was published but it does link somewhat to other things that were emerging in the world of psychoanalysis at the time (see the chapter on context).

The novel also suggests that the taking of drugs or, as Jekyll does in the novel, the taking of "powders" releases some sort of internal demon that isn't constrained by the rules that society has created. In *Jekyll and Hyde*, Hyde is physically deformed or somehow terrible to look at. This would link quite well to the Victorian notion that deformity or disfigurement somehow meant that a person was evil, that their inner deformity was visible on the outside. Victorians were terrified by the idea that they wouldn't know a person's true intent or character. The police at the time even compiled thousands and thousands of photographs of criminals and lower class people in the hope that studying them would reveal what a criminal or evil person looked like. The message to emerge from *Jekyll and Hyde*, that anyone can have a secret self, buried deep within until released, would have been very unsettling.

This novel then captures very well the idea of man being more than just one person or personality. It's a tale that still resonates today as we constantly battle with competing forces within us. The novel that both made Stevenson a star and a fortune and destroyed his reputation among friends and writers of the time as a "proper writer" is much more personal than many people at the time and since think. The double life that Stevenson himself led in Edinburgh, the influence of stories and characters from his childhood showing the two sides to people and the often subtle but nonetheless significant allusions to sex and sexuality, all point to a story that is much more "of" Robert Louis Stevenson than he, his wife or even his friends would care to admit.

Part 5: The setting

The Strange case of Dr Jekyll and Mr Hyde is set in the London of the late Victorian period - around the 1880s. It is, however, quite different to many other novels and stories set in London at this time (most notably the Sherlock Holmes tales). In many other stories, the city of London comes alive in the details descriptions and almost plays the role of a character in the story itself. In *Jekyll and Hyde* however, while there are descriptions that are most definitely London, there are, under the surface, striking resemblances to another British city. There is a long-held theory that the London of the novel is actually closer to Stevenson's home city of Edinburgh, with which he would have been much more familiar.

Both cities would have been smog-filled, dark and dangerous places in the late nineteenth century but there are certain aspects that are impossible to ignore that relate to events in the novel. At this time in Britain, many people moved from the countryside to the cities. London, in the 19th Century, was a city that had grown enormously in the space of 100 years. In the century from 1800 to 1900, London's population exploded. With roughly one million people living in the city at the beginning of the 19th Century, London's position as the capital of the British Empire made it attractive to immigrants from all of the empire's colonies. Within 100 years, the population had grown to nearly 7 million people - a hugely significant increase.

It's important to remember that this London of contrasts was home to people of significant and almost unimaginable wealth as well as to people dying of flu in overcrowded rooms, home to families of up to 20 people. Similarly, Edinburgh of Stevenson's youth was as divided and different as the two characters that make up the name of his novel. In today's Edinburgh there is the Old town and the New town. This 'New' town was built in the late 18th century as the upper classes and better off people of the city had grown tired of living so close to people of lower classes. The new part of the city was constructed within walking distance of the Old town but whereas the New town, where Stevenson grew up, had bright street lighting, wide streets and immaculately kept homes, the Old town was left to decay further. Here there were dangerous characters of all descriptions - thieves, drunks, prostitutes and murderers - all within walking distance of the respectable citizens of Edinburgh. It is this interesting facet of Edinburgh that leads many people to believe that while the action takes place in London, the story is really, at heart, from the winding alleyways and divided society of Edinburgh.

As we have seen in the chapter about the author, Stevenson became very familiar with the Old town of Edinburgh and would have mostly kept these activities secret. Just like many other upper class gentlemen who would have made the short walk from the New town to the Old to sample its darker atmosphere, Stevenson, in public, was a fine young man from a fine family who was set to be a great lawyer or engineer. Again, the dual nature, the double life is something that strikes a chord with Dr Jekyll in the novel.

Another fine gentleman from this period who Stevenson was very interested in and even wrote about but the story was never published, was a man called Deacon Brodie. Deacon William Brodie was an upstanding gentleman, a master craftsman who made cabinets and a city councilor. He had the title of Deacon as he was head of one of the city's trade guilds - a sort of association of craftsmen, which would have been a very important title to have in 18th century Britain. Because of his status, Brodie associated with all of the finest people in Edinburgh. He also repaired cabinets and the locks and mechanisms on them. He had access to the finest homes and wealthiest families in the city. All of this meant that he was the last person anyone suspected when there was a sudden increase in burglaries in all the finest homes in the city.

As it turned out, because of gambling debts he had incurred from spending his evenings in the Old town associating with criminals, Brodie needed money and considering he had such a good knowledge of the homes and the locks and cabinets of the richest people in the city - he took it from them. Again, the resemblance with *Jekyll and Hyde* is plain to see: a respectable gentleman by day, a dangerous criminal by night. The fact that Stevenson wrote a piece of work based on him is evidence enough to suggest that he had a big impact on the young man but also the fact that, in his bedroom as a child, there was one of Brodie's cabinets is also very interesting.

Much has been said and written about why Stevenson decided to set his story in London. Some say that he simply wanted the story to make more money. People in London would have been more interested in the story if it was set in the city they were from. This, however, is slightly less believable than another theory that further deepens the idea of the dual nature of man.

In London in the 18th century, there was a surgeon by the name of John Hunter. He was also known as "The Knife Man". He was a pioneering surgeon and made many discoveries. In order to develop his knowledge of human anatomy however, he had to do dissections. At this time, it was legal only for aspiring surgeons to carry out dissections on the dead bodies of criminals who had been executed. As with sexuality, Victorian society was squeamish about the idea of men cutting up decent gentlemen and women, even if they were already dead and even if it was for the pursuit of knowledge. This was a time of really quite rapid development in science and medicine (see the chapter on context for more on this) and if surgeons wanted to keep up, they had to have a good supply of bodies.

In Edinburgh at the time, two famous men - William Burke and William Hare - made a lot of money from digging up bodies that had recently been buried and selling them to a well-known surgeon in the city. This was, of course, entirely illegal but they made so much money that they decided that they would get them even fresher and began to murder people and bring the bodies around to the surgeon's home. Stevenson would have, again, been familiar with this story and even wrote a story about it himself called *The Bodysnatchers.*

The famous John Hunter in London may have been acquiring bodies in the same way but even the ones that were legal, the bodies of executed criminals, would have caused a stir if they were delivered to his front door - a respectable home in what is today Leicester Square. To combat this, he bought the house behind his own home and knocked down walls and built connecting corridors which meant that to the front, he had a beautiful, well-decorated home where he would entertain guests and enter and exit. To the rear he had built dissecting rooms and lecture theatres and, exiting out on to a very unfashionable and grotty Castle Street, he had the back door where the bodies were to be left in the morning.

Whether or not Stevenson had London or Edinburgh in mind for *Jekyll and Hyde,* it's clear that he has borrowed from both. Edinburgh itself is divided, a city with two personalities or faces - the respectable, upper class one and the lower, dangerous and illicit one. He also borrowed from John "The knife Man" Hunter the idea for Jekyll's home - a respectable front to something much darker and sinister. In fact, the description of Dr Jekyll's home in the story is so close to that of Hunter's that it must be more than coincidence.

Part 6: The context

Class

The 1800s in Britain was a time of great change. One of the most challenging things for the established upper classes in Victorian society was the influx of people viewed as working class or lower classes into the big cities of Britain. They were coming in search of work and housing but the cities of the time, especially London, were quite unprepared for them. The sudden increase in numbers made the upper classes nervous. They were clearly outnumbered and they began to create areas of these cities where they would not go and other areas where they would socialise. This division of the cities into "no-go areas" was interesting because it created an "other" in London specifically. Rich people tended to live in the west and stories of the debauchery and the goings on in places like the East End and Soho were both shocking and fascinating to them.

Many stories and novels from this time fall into the category of "shilling shockers". Stories that were written about these other people in order to shock, appall and entertain the upper classes. The lower classes about whom they were written were largely illiterate so they were not the intended audience. Stevenson's *Jekyll and Hyde* however, was written about the sort of upper class gentlemen whose wives would have read these "shilling shockers" and, as such, caused quite a stir. It was seen as typical of the lower classes to engage in this sort of behaviour (it was thought, for example, that there were thousands of prostitutes in the East End of London at the time the novel was published) but for a well-respected gentleman to have such a dark side to him was frightening.

The allegorical nature of the story was not lost on its audience at the time it was published either. Many saw the story as a morality tale of what can happen when you indulge or give in to your darker side. This is emphatically shown in the novel, as it is indeed the dark side that wins out and claims Jekyll. The nature of class is interesting in *Jekyll and Hyde* because there is no one really of the lower classes present in the story, except for, possibly Hyde himself.

Medical discoveries

Science and medicine were also changing quickly at this time in history. As we have seen in earlier chapters, famous surgeons were experimenting and dissecting bodies to learn all they could about human anatomy. The first transplants were carried out around this time too by men such as John Hunter. Hunter conducted bizarre experiments where he grafted a human tooth onto a chicken's head to see if it would grow, as well as many other experiments. This notion of the "mad scientist" shocked the public and many of the experiments were carried out in secret and their results shared among respected members of the profession in private houses around Britain.

These themes are also carried through to *Jekyll and Hyde* where we see Dr Jekyll in his London home with his labs and powders locked away with his research. He begins to experiment on himself (which John Hunter is also reputed to have done) and soon, he gets into a situation he can't handle. This was a common fear of the Victorian age - of discovering something shocking or creating something monstrous (think *Frankenstein*) that would overpower us and destroy us.

Clearly Stevenson is addressing these concerns only this time, instead of it being a creation, or something terrible from the East End of London like in most of the "shilling shockers" of the day, in this case the monster comes from within. It already exists. All that is required is some medical marvel to unleash it and destroy it's other, better, half.

The development of psychoanalysis

Stevenson, according to his wife, read many reports, mostly from France, of the growing field of psychoanalysis and dream analysis. He was obsessed with dreams, their meanings and their relation to our subconscious selves (or the "other fellow" as Stevenson christened his other self). Stevenson's wife even went so far as to claim that the seed for *Jekyll and Hyde* actually came from a French scientific journal. Stevenson said that he had read a scientific article about a young Frenchman who had developed a case where he would have dramatic and severe personality shifts as a result of a severe shock but he maintained that he had read that account after the publication of *Jekyll and Hyde*.

It's difficult to resist seeing many parallels with the work of Sigmund Freud, the most famous psychoanalysts and the man who is seen as the father of psychoanalysis. Freud was a few years younger than Stevenson but it is very likely that they would have been reading the same journals and articles and so, would have been exposed to the same ideas. Some of Stevenson's ideas predate Freud's, especially those of the duality of man, but their similarities are very clear.

Freud's theories cover the ideas of the subconscious and how the conscious self (the public self) covers up the desires and wishes of the subconscious (the private self) until, as we grow older, we completely forget the subconscious. He is able, according to his
research, to access a patient's subconscious through dialogue and, in many cases, able to identify and locate the cause of some illness of the present in the patient's past - usually a suppressed and covered up event in childhood.

As an Austrian, Freud would not have necessarily shared the Victorians' general aversion to anything related to sex and, as such, many of his theories relate to the repression of sexuality and sexual inclination. Again, this is something that appears to be central to our understanding of *Jekyll and Hyde*.

Similarly, another book published at the time and one that was entirely shocking yet widely talked about was *Psychopathia Sexualis* written by another European, Richard Von Krafft-Ebing. His book was a study of sexual behaviour in people and included many case studies and interviews. To the Victorian society for which any talk of sexuality was completely forbidden or spoken about in metaphors and knowing glances, this was a treasure-trove of information to be appalled by. That it was published around the same time as *Jekyll and Hyde* and that *Jekyll and Hyde* was subtle enough to leave most of the details up to the imaginations of its readers means that *Jekyll and Hyde* took on a very new meaning (possibly many different and conflicting meanings) in readers' minds.

Jekyll and Hyde then is a book of its time. It was a time when medicine was about to unveil the inner mysteries of human anatomy, when psychoanalysis was about to unveil the inner mysteries of the human mind and human sexuality and also a time when class and political tensions were threatening the established status quo, the cosy consensus that had existed for the upper classes for decades. To say that the Victorians were neither ready nor equipped for all these changes is an understatement. In this context, *Jekyll and Hyde* emerges to shock, fascinate and hold a mirror up to the people who were reading it.

Part 7: Character analysis – Dr. Henry Jekyll

Dr Henry Jekyll is a well-respected scientist who is famous for his intellect, his gentlemanly qualities and his dinner parties. At these parties, we learn, there are usually men "all intelligent and reputable" and also, all "judges of good wine". Jekyll, then, is a member of the upper classes who is liked by his peers and used to the finer things in life.

Jekyll is a man of fifty who is "large, well-made, smooth-faced…[with] every mark of capacity and kindness". Stevenson, in his first presentation of Jekyll is sure to present him as a character for whom we have positive feelings. He is shown to be the kind, generous Victorian gentleman. He has recently made out a will that is being kept by the lawyer, Mr Utterson. Utterson, however, is disturbed by the will because Jekyll has decided that, should he die, he wants to leave his considerable fortune to a man by the name of Mr Hyde.

In his "statement of the case" (chapter 10) we learn that Henry Jekyll was born "to a large fortune" and had a thoroughly good upbringing. He was "inclined by nature to industry, fond of the respect of the wise and good among my fellow-men, and thus, as might have been supposed, with every guarantee of an honourable and distinguished future". In short, Jekyll is the perfect Victorian gentleman. He's from a good family and, to anyone looking at him from outside, he would have been almost guaranteed a good future.

Here, however, Stevenson introduces this idea of the double life. He tells us that "the worst of [his] faults was a certain impatient gaiety of disposition" which attempted to trivialise his indiscretions in his younger years. He goes on to give a closer idea of what he got up to as a young man when he says that he hid these "irregularities" with an almost "morbid sense of shame". The suggestion here is that his activities as a younger man were sexual in nature and, although not specified directly (remember, Stevenson's wife objected to the first draft being too explicit) it's interesting to remember that homosexuality was still a crime in Victorian society.

Jekyll hides and represses these youthful indiscretions and says that he "concealed his pleasures" for the sake of his career and standing in society. It is these indiscretions that Utterson thinks Hyde is using to blackmail Jekyll into leaving him all his possessions. In covering up his youthful activities, Jekyll says that he came to realise the "profound duplicity of life". He begins to develop a theory or idea of how one might separate these two personalities - the good side and the bad side. In his experiments, he develops a potion that, when drunk, transforms Henry Jekyll into Edward Hyde.

An interesting point to make here is that this novel is not simply a story about good versus evil as it's often made out to be. While Edward Hyde is a distillation of pure evil, Henry Jekyll isn't all good. He admits that within himself he often fights his desires and compulsions in order to conform to Victorian society. He is a mixed character and when he takes the potion, he must have had some element of evil in him to create Hyde. He says himself that "had [he] approached [his] discovery in a more noble spirit, had [he] risked the experiment while under the empire of generous or pious aspirations, all must have been otherwise, and from [the experiment] … come forth an angel instead of a fiend".

What Jekyll is saying here is that he was looking for an excuse or a way to carry out these "concealed pleasures" of his when he took the potion and, from that beginning, was spawned Hyde. If he had been good in his intentions, the creature that he transformed into would have been good. So, rather than the potion separating good from evil, it can be viewed as distilling and separating true desires. Again, when read in Victorian times, this idea would have been very unsettling, especially given the added sexual undertones.

Ultimately, Jekyll is too weak to contain Hyde. At first, he intends to use Hyde to fulfil his pleasures. He tells the servants of his own house that the man, Edward Hyde, is to be allowed full access to the house and not to be spoken to. He also sets up an apartment for Hyde in Soho, one of the seedier areas of London at the time, and continues to take the potion to transform into Hyde and then, in the morning, change back into the respectable Dr Henry Jekyll.

Over time, Hyde begins to appear when *he* wants to. Jekyll loses control. This is one of the most troubling allegories of the story. Is Stevenson saying here that if we give in to our darker sides that they will ultimately end up winning out over our good? Or, is he saying that to repress and conceal these sides to ourselves is to hide who we are and damage ourselves psychologically? It's clear that Jekyll is in many ways horrified by his own actions when he's transformed into Hyde but he continues to go back to his rooms and take the potion. At one point in the novel, Dr Jekyll assures Mr Utterson that there is nothing to worry about and, if he wished, Hyde would disappear never to return. We come to realise that this isn't true and, in fact, echoes the words of many addicts before and since.

Part 8: Character analysis – Mr. Edward Hyde

Mr Edward Hyde is described to us many times in the novel and yet, despite that, there's a certain fluid nature to him; he can't necessarily be captured. The only constant between each of the characters who encounter him is that they feel a physical revulsion, an overwhelming sense of badness and evil. Unlike Jekyll, Hyde is unable to hide who he is and what he represents.

Hyde is first described by Enfield, Utterson's walking companion. In contrast to Jekyll, who is described in glowing and positive terms, Hyde is first described trampling a young girl on the pavement and leaving her screaming in agony. Physically he is described not like a man, but "like some damned Juggernaut". Enfield tells us that when they caught him, he was "perfectly cool" but gave him "one look, so ugly that it brought out a sweat" on him. He furthers his description by telling us that he "had taken a loathing to him at first sight" and that another man there, a doctor, "turned sick and white with the desire to kill him" every time he caught sight of him.

Enfield tells Utterson of the house where Hyde entered and came out of (the back door to the home of Henry Jekyll) and refers to it as "Blackmail House" as he believes Henry Jekyll to be "an honest man paying through the nose for some of the capers of his youth".

The descriptions of Hyde are very interesting and the language that Stevenson uses is also quite telling. When Utterson finally catches up with Hyde and approaches him, Hyde shrinks back from him "with a hissing intake of breath". Hyde is often described in animalistic terms. He is presented as not fully formed (he walks with a limp, appears young and is short) which could represent that the evil or dark side of Jekyll was when he was a younger man or it could also mean that he's not yet fully formed in his evil ways. Just like a newborn animal takes time to adjust to the world, the newborn Hyde is getting used to his surroundings.

We see that, when talking with a gentleman, Hyde does not use "fitting language" and at one point in his conversation with Utterson, he "snarled aloud into a savage laugh". Stevenson is presenting a character who is almost animal-like in his reactions and interactions and when he is described visually, he is "pale and dwarfish" with a "broken voice" and altogether "hardly human". All who meet Hyde find that his "unpleasantness" is infections and he inspires in people "a nausea and distaste for life".

Stevenson could be trying to suggest through the character of Hyde that our subconscious (see context) is more primal and closer to nature than our conscious selves are. This recalls Freud's work on the subconscious and the primal, subconscious motives that drive us. Stevenson may be hinting that, for all our civilisation and all the strict rules of Victorian society, underneath the polish, all of us harbour some of these more animalistic, base actions.

When Hyde murders Sir Danvers Carew his actions are shown to have much more of an impact than just on the murdered man. Hyde's actions are suggested to be depraved and perverted but only the trampling of the young girl at the beginning and the murder of Sir Danvers Carew are described to the reader in any detail. The other indiscretions are left up to the reader's imagination. In the case of the murder, it is suggested that Hyde, for no reason, responds to Carew's 'good evening' by attacking him with his cane.

The words of the eye-witness are important because it allows us to see some of the themes and ideas of class (see context) reflected in the world of the novel. According to the witness, Carew bows and approaches Hyde with "a pretty manner of politeness". The witness describes Carew's face as "innocent" and having an "old-world kindness of disposition". Once she looks at Hyde however, she "conceived a dislike" and goes on to describe how Hyde "carried on like a madman", attacking Carew with "an ape-like fury" and showing "insensate cruelty".

Here Carew represents the upper-class of Victorian London. The "old-world kindness" refers to the established values among the Victorian class who were nervous and worried about the influx of others not like them into London, for fear their way of life would be altered or overtaken. Hyde represents the other, with an animalistic and violent fury, he smashes this old way of life to pieces and it is a crime, we are told, that "startled London" and that it was even more notable "by the high position of the victim". Hyde's actions here have shaken an entire city and destroyed its peace.

Hyde represents the dangerous elements of London in the Victorian period. He lives and "socialises" in Soho, one of the places to which respectable Victorians would not have ventured (publicly at least) and his actions are not tempered or constrained either by the rule of law or by what society expects of him. In many ways, Hyde is the only character in the story who is actually true to himself. He is mostly evil and he acts on this evil without thinking. All of the other characters mediate their thoughts and feelings through what is right or what is thought to be right.

Part 9: Character analysis – Mr. Utterson

Stevenson presents Mr Utterson very carefully in the opening pages of the novel for a number of reasons. Firstly, much of the action is seen through Utterson's eyes and, because its subject matter is quite unbelievable, it's crucial that Stevenson make him as *believable* as possible. To do this he presents him first and foremost as a lawyer, a man who is professional and used to strange and peculiar cases. He also makes him a very serious character. We are told that he "was never lighted by a smile; cold scanty and embarrassed in discourse; backward in sentiment; lean, long, dusty, dreary, and yet somehow lovable".

This description is Stevenson through and through. He sets up his character as someone very serious, dry, not prone to smiling but then at the end turns it on its head by using the adjective "lovable". This encourages a positive response to Utterson from the reader and, having established that he's serious and not prone to any extremes of personality (probably the complete opposite of Dr Jekyll) he then goes on to embellish or decorate his character with some positive traits.

We learn that "when the wine was to his taste, something eminently human beaconed from his eye". But, in case we think that he drinks too much, we are reminded that he is "austere with himself" and, although he likes the theatre, he hasn't "crossed the doors of one for twenty years". Despite the fact that he is strict with himself and doesn't go in for frivolities like the theatre, we also learn something very important - he's tolerant of other people. He has always been "inclined to help rather than reprove" and goes along with a saying of his own: "I let my brother go to the devil in his own way".

This makes Mr Utterson quite a unique character. He represents much of the ideals of the Victorian gentleman - he is serious yet human, tolerant of others but strict with himself - but he is contrast to a character such as Henry Jekyll, as he is not thought to have the dual nature within him. Also, his tolerance is quite interesting. As a Victorian, there were lots of things considered to be wrong or outside of the rules of society. Sex and sexuality were repressed and not spoken of; homosexuality was illegal and despised. Men and women filled very clear and defined roles and children too were expected to behave according to their class. To be tolerant was something that would not have been shared universally across Victorian society.

It is important, however, that Utterson is all of these things because, as we said at the beginning, he needs to be a serious man so that we can believe his version of events, regardless of how shocking or strange they are. Similarly, he needs to be tolerant because he needs to be the one that Jekyll will open up to about his strange experiences. There is really no one else who could fulfil that role in the story. Finally, he needs to be trustworthy but not interesting in himself so that he doesn't distract too much from the other characters of the story.

He fills these roles very well and is, in fact, the perfect character through whom to see the world of the novel. He is not judgmental (which allows the reader to decide certain things for themselves), he is trusting of what others tell him (which allows the reader to take these reports on their own merits) and he is tolerant of others (which allows Jekyll to tell him and the reader the events of the story). In short, he is the perfect foil to show off the other characters' differences and contrasts.

Part 10: Stevenson's use of language

One of the difficulties for any Victorian writer, who had to stick to very strict rules about decency and decorum, was how to describe things in a way that would shock the reader but also allow them to fill in the blanks with things that, often, were even more horrific than what the writer intended. Journalists at the time of the Whitechapel murders, or the Jack the Ripper murders as they are more commonly known, were prohibited from describing the actual details of the deaths of the women involved as it would have broken the decency laws of the time and be seen as pornographic.

As such, Stevenson had to use language in a very particular way to create an atmosphere of dread and horror without being too graphic or explicit. Similarly, when describing dreadful things, he often uses language which communicates the shocking nature of the event even though the language used is oddly formal and very much of the Victorian period. For example, when Hyde's trampling of the young girl is described, the fact that such formal language is used almost makes it even more shocking.

As he retells the events to Utterson, Enfield says that he watched Hyde and the young girl approaching the same corner but from different directions. The language used to describe the event itself is interesting. "Well, Sir, the two ran into one another naturally enough at the corner" and "the man trampled calmly over the child's body and left her screaming on the ground". Stevenson's use of the word "trampled" is vague enough for us to come up with our own vision of what has happened but also the use of the adverb "calmly" implies that there was something terrible about the man and it allows us to put together a picture of both the man and the event without too much interference of the author's description.

It is a quite effective technique of introducing ambiguity but also signposts such as "calmly" "trampled" that force us to create our own image. In fact, the very next line bears this out. Enfield says that "it sounds nothing to hear, but it was hellish to see". This duality or double nature of the language used - the shocking being described in such formal tones - is reflective of the story itself and its main character. It's also linked to the way language is used in other ways in the story.

Stevenson uses contrast - highlighting the difference between two things - in a very fitting way for a story about the two different personalities within a man. In his setting of the scene, Stevenson repeatedly uses contrast to emphasise the frightening and to create a dark atmosphere and tone. When describing Enfield and Utterson's Sunday walk, he prefaces his description of the location of the mystery by discussing what's around it. We are told that the inhabitants of the area are all "doing well" and hoping to do "better still". The street itself "shone out in contrast to its dingy neighborhood, like a fire in a forest". Ultimately, just before we come to the scene of the crime (so to speak) Stevenson gives us a long, rambling sentence about the beauty and charming nature of the area:

"…With its freshly painted shutters, well-polished brasses, and general cleanliness and gaiety of note, instantly caught and pleased the eye of the passenger."

This allows the next piece of information to have more impact - how could there possibly be anything negative in such a lovely environment? But there is:

"Two doors from one corner, on the left hand going east, the line was broken by the entry of a court; and just at that point, a certain sinister block of building thrust forward its gable in the street."

As well as the use of alliteration to emphasise the "**c**ertain **s**inister **b**lock of **b**uilding", Stevenson also uses personification to imply that the house is somehow able to "thrust" itself out onto the pavement creating the impression of a house or building that personifies the evil within Hyde himself.

The rest of that passage is worth looking at in detail to examine how Stevenson carefully builds an atmosphere in direct contrast to what has gone before. This allows the building, upon which the story centres, to stand out from its surroundings. The building is not pleasant though it is surrounded by things that are. We could link this idea to Henry Jekyll who surrounds himself with gentlemen of good standing even though he himself has a terrible secret to hide.

"It was two storeys and had a blind forehead of discoloured wall on the upper; and bore in every feature the marks of prolonged and sordid negligence. The door, which was equipped with neither bell nor knocker, was blistered and distained. Tramps slouched into the recess and struck matches on the panels; children kept shop upon the steps; the schoolboy had tried his knife on the mouldings; and for close on a generation no one had appeared to drive on these random visitors or to repair their ravages."

Stevenson is so detailed in his attempt to set this location up for the reader as somehow dangerous and sinister. At the beginning it's almost as if he's trying to personify the building with its "blind forehead". Is it "blind" because it does not want to see what is going on inside or outside its walls? We are told that the walls are "discoloured" - no one is looking after its upkeep. It's the next sentence that is particularly interesting however. The word "sordid" is usually used to suggest something that is morally objectionable. Is the suggestion here that the buildings occupants are the ones who have committed the "sordid negligence" and, if so, what is the sordid nature of their actions?

Although we don't know yet who lives here, only that it is connected with the story Enfield is telling Utterson about Hyde, the cumulative effect of this sort of language is to create an atmosphere suited to the revealing of a mystery and sets the reader up for the events that follow.

Considering Stevenson's fascination with dreams and what he believed them to reveal about people's subconscious, the appearance of a dream sequence or even a dream-like sequence within the novel itself should be read very carefully. And it is in such a sequence that we get one of the best descriptions of London in the entire novel.

In one such dream when Utterson lay "tossed in the gross darkness of the room" he sees a "great field of lamps of a nocturnal city". His dream from here on becomes infected with the presence of a dark and sinister shape however, and he sees this shape "glide more stealthily…through wider labyrinths of lamp-lighted city". The idea of the labyrinth or maze and the narrow, lamp-lit streets and alleyways of London evoke a very sinister and haunting atmosphere for the reader.

When Utterson finally catches up with Hyde, the atmosphere too is important. It is to be their first meeting and it takes place at night "under the face of the fogged city moon". Stevenson describes the "low growl of London" personifying the city once again as something animalistic or threatening. When he comes face-to-face with Hyde, he ultimately concludes that the man "is hardly human". (For a look at the language used to describe Hyde by the characters who discuss him see Character analysis - Mr Edward Hyde).

One final aspect of language to examine is the symbolic nature of the house and laboratory of Henry Jekyll. As we've seen above, the exterior of the house is described in great detail to develop its sinister nature but it's also important to remember that the house represents both Dr Jekyll and Mr Hyde (for more on the setting see Setting). The warren and labyrinth of streets around the back entrance, described so atmospherically above, prevented people from connecting that entrance to the property with Dr Jekyll's front door around on another side and accessible from a different street. This represents the relationship between the two characters and also how it's difficult for anyone to put them together. Utterson himself is unable to do this until the very end when all is revealed.

Part 11: Stevenson's use of structure & form

If the language used by Stevenson in his *Jekyll and Hyde* reflects the theme of duality within the novel and of its main character, then the structure goes even further. Firstly, to the title itself - *The Strange case of Dr Jekyll and Mr Hyde*. The title gives the impression that some sort of study or formal report is contained within the pages. As mentioned earlier (context) Stevenson had been reading scientific and psychoanalytic articles and journals at the time, detailing "strange cases" and, as such, his title here reflects the scientific or medical nature within. It also serves to completely disarm the reader as they actually encounter something very different to a formal, scientific text. Of course, this only applies to a first time reader who has no knowledge of Jekyll and Hyde being the same character, a very rare thing nowadays.

Firstly, let's look at the overall structure of the story. For more detailed information on Freytag's pyramid, check out Mr Bruff's guide to *Frankenstein*. Here, we can look at the general structure for any piece of work:

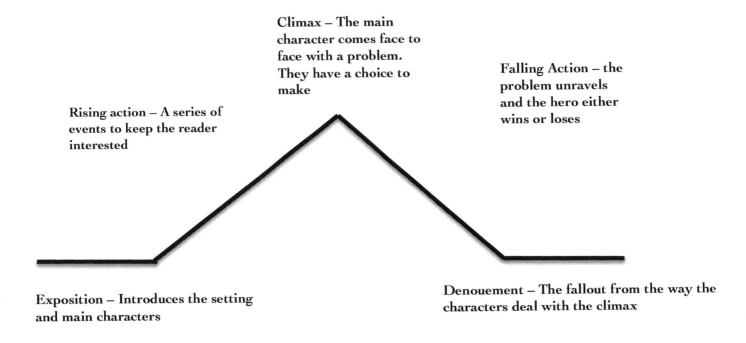

Climax – The main character comes face to face with a problem. They have a choice to make

Falling Action – the problem unravels and the hero either wins or loses

Rising action – A series of events to keep the reader interested

Exposition – Introduces the setting and main characters

Denouement – The fallout from the way the characters deal with the climax

And here we see the *Jekyll and Hyde* fitting quite easily:

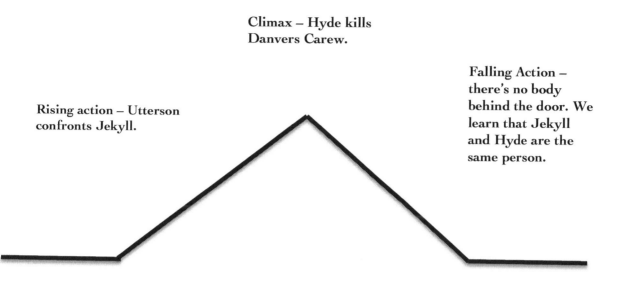

Climax – Hyde kills
Danvers Carew.

Falling Action –
there's no body
behind the door. We
learn that Jekyll
and Hyde are the
same person.

Rising action – Utterson
confronts Jekyll.

Exposition – We meet Mr Utterson
and his friend Enfield. We learn that
Utterson is unhappy about Jekyll
leaving his money to Hyde.

Denouement – Jekyll and Hyde are both
dead.

Narrative structure

In terms of narrative structure, *Jekyll and Hyde* uses a number of different types specifically to build up the tension in the story. There are three distinct parts or sections to the novel. The first eight chapters are from the point of view of Mr Utterson, the ninth chapter from the point of view of Dr Lanyon (a friend of both Utterson and Jekyll) and the tenth chapter is from the perspective of Dr Jekyll himself. *Jekyll and Hyde,* then, is a multiple narrative novel. It's also non-linear, meaning that the events that take place are not related to the reader in the order in which they take place. For example, once we have switched focus from Mr Utterson to Dr Lanyon in chapter nine, the action goes backwards, to events that we've already covered, but seen from another perspective.

This is interesting for a number of reasons. Firstly, it echoes the assumptions one might have made based on the title - this is the testimony or witness statement of three different characters. It would be expected in any case study that the opinions and ideas of more than one witness would be included. Secondly, it reflects the subject matter of the novel itself very well. There's more than one "voice" or "personality" at work in the novel and it's entirely up to us which one we pay most attention to or believe the most. The duality of the central character, Dr Jekyll, is reflected in the multiple voices or personalities within the novel.

Stevenson opens the tale using a third person narrative through the eyes of the lawyer, Mr Utterson. This is not accidental. As we've seen previously (see Character analysis - Mr Utterson) Mr Utterson is a very balanced and serious individual who is not someone who jumps to conclusions or gets carried away. This, in turn, means that we see the world as he does. He approaches the events in a rational, non-emotional manner and we tend to follow suit. Utterson is a "safe" character and one who we would not imagine would become frightened or nervous easily. This, however, makes the subsequent events even more shocking as it's something that, considering the way we've been introduced to this world, we would not have expected at all.

He is in the dark for most of the novel about the true events taking place. Because we are restricted to his view, we too are in the dark and can only share his suspicions about the will, about Mr Hyde and about the afflictions Dr Jekyll is suffering from. Most of the opening eight chapters are concerned with Utterson's theories and hypotheses. As a lawyer, he's someone used to taking the facts and combining them with his own opinions and attempting to come up with an explanation. This use of the third person narrative from Utterson's perspective forces us to distance ourselves from the actual events taking place with Jekyll and Hyde. We are observers looking in from the outside trying to figure it out.

Stevenson then does something interesting, however. When he introduces Dr Lanyon's narrative he writes in first person, in the form of a letter. The use of first person narrative removes this distance from the events and forces us to be up close and personal with Dr Jekyll's struggle. It also forces us make a judgement on Jekyll, on whether or not he is the victim that he appears to present himself as. The fact that the first person narrator is Dr Lanyon, a friend of Jekyll, makes it easier to feel sympathy towards him as he is viewed by the narrator with sympathetic eyes. Another important fact here is that the writer, Dr Lanyon, is dead so there are no further questions that can be asked; there can be no further discussion. It's a closed source.

The third narrative is also written in the first person and it is a first hand account from Dr Henry Jekyll himself. This narrative is the closing chapter and, as such, puts an end to the case. Its title too is interesting: *Henry Jekyll's full statement of the case*. Here the non-linear nature of the novel is emphasised again as we go even further back when Jekyll's discussing his upbringing and also his first attempts to distill this potion that could separate the good and the bad sides of people. This narrative reads almost like a confession (a type of writing which was very popular at this time in both prose and poetry) where Jekyll is appealing to the readers to understand *his* side of the story. It's hard not to feel sympathy and to do as Jekyll seems to be asking: to see him as the victim of his youth and the society in which he lives.

The combined effect of these narratives is that the novel itself feels fractured, like it is more than one thing, until you get to the end when all of the pieces come together to make perfect sense. Stevenson structures *Jekyll and Hyde* in this way to create and then build the tension. It's like he has a curtain, half drawn, over the story and he is revealing it very slowly and then going a few steps backwards and then revealing even more before, finally, giving us the truth of it. It's a very effective technique and made even more impressive by Stevenson's tight control.

Sentence structure

Finally, let's take a look at some of the ways that Stevenson structures language on the sentence and paragraph level. Consider this passage where Jekyll describes waking up as Hyde. Pay close attention to how Stevenson carefully structures his writing to take the reader on a journey from Jekyll's mind to Hyde's body and how the normal and commonplace gradually turn into horror and panic:

Some two months before the murder of Sir Danvers, I had been out for one of my adventures, had returned at a late hour, and woke the next day in bed with somewhat odd sensations. It was in vain I looked about me; in vain I saw the decent furniture and tall proportions of my room in the square; in vain that I recognised the pattern of the bed-curtains and the design of the mahogany frame; something still kept insisting that I was not where I was, that I had not wakened where I seemed to be, but in the little room in Soho where I was accustomed to sleep in the body of Edward Hyde. I smiled to myself, and, in my psychological way began lazily to inquire into the elements of this illusion, occasionally, even as I did so, dropping back into a comfortable morning doze. I was still so engaged when, in one of my more wakeful moments, my eyes fell upon my hand. Now the hand of Henry Jekyll (as you have often remarked) was professional in shape and size: it was large, firm, white, and comely. But the hand which I now saw, clearly enough, in the yellow light of a mid-London morning, lying half shut on the bed-clothes, was lean, corded, knuckly, of a dusky pallor and thickly shaded with a swart growth of hair. **It was the hand of Edward Hyde.**

Consider the length of the underlined sentence. Here we have our narrator waking up with "odd sensations". This is placed at the end of the first sentence in the passage, setting us up for what is about to come next. The suspense is built gradually and slowly as we read that Jekyll carries out all these morning tasks "in vain" before making the calm decision that this was the room where he was "accustomed to sleep in the body of Edward Hyde". This calm acceptance comes at the end of a long, rambling sentence perhaps reflecting the rambling thoughts of a man who has just woken up.

The next sentence too is long and uses multiple phrases and clauses separated by commas to enhance the sensation of laziness, relaxation and sleepiness. That is until he begins to wake up and become more aware of the "hand which I now saw, clearly enough, in the yellow light of a mid-London morning" which he comes to realise is the hand of none other than Edward Hyde. Notice the sentence in bold and compare it in length to the other sentences Stevenson uses. This combination of long, lazy and rambling sentences lulls the reader into a false sense of security. We are almost dozing like Jekyll is. The short sentence at the end leaves us in no doubt, however, that something is terribly wrong and its length emphasises the danger.

Part 12: Sample questions & answers

EXTRACT FOR Q1

Some two months before the murder of Sir Danvers, I had been out for one of my adventures, had returned at a late hour, and woke the next day in bed with somewhat odd sensations. It was in vain I looked about me; in vain I saw the decent furniture and tall proportions of my room in the square; in vain that I recognised the pattern of the bed-curtains and the design of the mahogany frame; something still kept insisting that I was not where I was, that I had not wakened where I seemed to be, but in the little room in Soho where I was accustomed to sleep in the body of Edward Hyde. I smiled to myself, and, in my psychological way began lazily to inquire into the elements of this illusion, occasionally, even as I did so, dropping back into a comfortable morning doze. I was still so engaged when, in one of my more wakeful moments, my eyes fell upon my hand. Now the hand of Henry Jekyll (as you have often remarked) was professional in shape and size: it was large, firm, white, and comely. But the hand which I now saw, clearly enough, in the yellow light of a mid-London morning, lying half shut on the bed-clothes, was lean, corded, knuckly, of a dusky pallor and thickly shaded with a swart growth of hair. It was the hand of Edward Hyde.

I must have stared upon it for near half a minute, sunk as I was in the mere stupidity of wonder, before terror woke up in my breast as sudden and startling as the crash of cymbals; and bounding from my bed, I rushed to the mirror. At the sight that met my eyes, my blood was changed into something exquisitely thin and icy. Yes, I had gone to bed Henry Jekyll, I had awakened Edward Hyde. How was this to be explained? I asked myself, and then, with another bound of terror—how was it to be remedied? It was well on in the morning; the servants were up; all my drugs were in the cabinet—a long journey down two pairs of stairs, through the back passage, across the open court and through the anatomical theatre, from where I was then standing horror-struck. It might indeed be possible to cover my face; but of what use was that, when I was unable to conceal the alteration in my stature? And then with an overpowering sweetness of relief, it came back upon my mind that the servants were already used to the coming and going of my second self. I had soon dressed, as well as I was able, in clothes of my own size: had

41

soon passed through the house, where Bradshaw stared and drew back at seeing Mr. Hyde at such an hour and in such a strange array; and ten minutes later, Dr. Jekyll had returned to his own shape and was sitting down, with a darkened brow, to make a feint of breakfasting.

Q1) How does Stevenson make this moment such a fascinating one in the novel?

A1) Stevenson makes this moment in the novel such a fascinating one by using vivid imagery to describe the unexpected change from Dr. Jekyll to Mr. Hyde. Also, this moment is very fascinating and revealing to the reader because we can finally see Hyde getting more powerful which could be a premonition to him nearly taking over completely later on in the novel.

Stevenson makes this moment in the novel fantastic by highly contrasting the hands of Dr. Jekyll and Mr. Hyde, symbolizing the differences between the Victorian Gentleman and the degenerate beings that swarm the darker parts of London:

'The hand of Henry Jekyll … was professional in shape and size; it was large, firm, white and comely … but the hand which I now saw … was lean, corded, knuckly, of a dusky pallor … with a swart growth of hair'

The contrasting description of the two hands is shown in this passage and symbolizes the duality of man, which we can see is a reoccurring theme throughout the novella. Jekyll's hand is described as 'large' and 'firm' which is a reflection of his own body as he is presented as a large and welcoming figure. This highlights his positive attributes, which is what is expected of a gentleman in restrictive Victorian society. His 'white' and 'comely' hand represents his purity and his goodwill; he would never harm another human being and his 'comely' appearance strengthens his approachability and his highly regarded position in society, which he strongly sought after. But representing the darker 'id' of ourselves is the description of Hyde's hand which depicts the gloomier side of humanity. This sudden change in description makes this moment extremely fantastic. The hand is described as 'lean' and 'corded', which conveys the small yet strong side to Jekyll's soul. The 'growth' of 'hair' likens Hyde to some primordial ape, which would shock the Victorian readers who believe they are made in God's image and are not evolved from apes. This represents humanity's bestial nature and signifies how Stevenson's trying to fight the duality of man will have severe consequences. The effects of this adamant behaviour on splitting the soul are seen earlier in the novella when Jekyll wakes up as Hyde without any otherworld potion, which marks the dark descent of Jekyll turning irreversibly into Hyde. The physical alterations are repeatedly mentioned throughout the novel, usually describing Hyde as having some unknown 'deformity'. The differences between the two parts of Jekyll are extremely strange and fantastic for the reader.

Furthermore, Jekyll's reaction makes this moment fantastic as it is very dramatic and it emphasizes the unexpected nature of this transformation.

'As sudden and startling as a crash of cymbals... bounding from my bed...my blood was changed into something exquisitely thin and icy'

This moment is very fantastic as the reader's disgust and shock is matched by Jekyll's own dramatic reaction when his 'blood' changed into 'ic[e]'. This metaphor greatly augments the horror of this unexpected transformation and how it is getting harder for Jekyll to control the beast within. The repetition of 'bounding' also emphasizes the shock that Jekyll felt when he realised he'd transformed without the use of some otherworldly potion. The 'crash' of 'cymbals' also augment the suddenness of this change and it allows the reader to think that Hyde is growing stronger and soon will gain control, due to Jekyll's stubbornness when he doesn't accept Hyde as part of himself and continues trying to get rid of him altogether. This is fantastic as the reader realises that the 'id' is part of the human soul and trying to split it is breaking apart the duality of man and will have severe consequences. These sudden changes are also seen earlier in the novel when we are shown that he has changed in the middle of a park, in broad daylight, due to vain thoughts.

Additionally, the contrasting atmospheres in this passage further the fantastic nature of this passage by strengthening the readers' and Jekyll's shock of the unexpected change from Jekyll to Hyde:

"I smiled to myself...dropping back into a comfortable morning doze...terror woke up in my breast...bound of terror."

Stevenson make this moment very exhilarating by contrasting the two atmospheres in the passage through imagery and description. Firstly, Jekyll is described to have 'smiled' to himself, which has connotations of extreme happiness and comfort. This could represent the exterior, superficial Victorian gentlemen ideals. This is augmented when Jekyll 'dropp[ed]...into' a 'morning doze' which shows us that Jekyll has no worries at all, and he can calmly go to sleep. This is directly contrasted when Jekyll's 'terror woke up' inside him. This completely destroys the idea of the Victorian gentleman as it is the exact opposite of a 'doze'. This suggests that there is a darker, more evil, bestial nature inside everyone. This moment of self-discovery is fantastic for the reader. This is further amplified by his 'bound of terror'. The dynamic verb of 'bound' accentuates the contrast between a 'comfortable' rest and a terror stricken panic. It also has connotations of an animalistic nature as it conjures up the image of a primordial degenerate 'bound[ing]' from a cage. These two atmospheres could represent the duality of man, portrayed as the accepted Victorian gentleman, and the feared 'id' of our inner self and our true nature. This theme of duality is seen throughout the novel, including the description of London itself, the rich 'fire' in the forest and the lowlife degenerates who live in the poorer parts.

"Ay, ay," said the lawyer. "My fears incline to the same point. Evil, I fear, founded—evil was sure to come—of that connection. Ay, truly, I believe you; I believe poor Harry is killed; and I believe his murderer (for what purpose, God alone can tell) is still lurking in his victim's room. Well, let our name be vengeance. Call Bradshaw."

The footman came at the summons, very white and nervous.

"Pull yourself together, Bradshaw," said the lawyer. "This suspense, I know, is telling upon all of you; but it is now our intention to make an end of it. Poole, here, and I are going to force our way into the cabinet. If all is well, my shoulders are broad enough to bear the blame. Meanwhile, lest anything should really be amiss, or any malefactor seek to escape by the back, you and the boy must go round the corner with a pair of good sticks and take your post at the laboratory door. We give you ten minutes to get to your stations."

As Bradshaw left, the lawyer looked at his watch. "And now, Poole, let us get to ours," he said; and taking the poker under his arm, led the way into the yard. The scud had banked over the moon, and it was now quite dark. The wind, which only broke in puffs and draughts into that deep well of building, tossed the light of the candle to and fro about their steps, until they came into the shelter of the theatre, where they sat down silently to wait. London hummed solemnly all around; but nearer at hand, the stillness was only broken by the sounds of a footfall moving to and fro along the cabinet floor.

"So it will walk all day, sir," whispered Poole; "ay, and the better part of the night. Only when a new sample comes from the chemist, there's a bit of a break. Ah, it's an ill conscience that's such an enemy to rest! Ah, sir, there's blood foully shed in every step of it! But hark again, a little closer—put your heart in your ears, Mr. Utterson, and tell me, is that the doctor's foot?"

The steps fell lightly and oddly, with a certain swing, for all they went so slowly; it was different indeed from the heavy creaking tread of Henry Jekyll. Utterson sighed. "Is there never anything else?" he asked.

Poole nodded. "Once," he said. "Once I heard it weeping!"

"Weeping? how that?" said the lawyer, conscious of a sudden chill of horror.

"Weeping like a woman or a lost soul," said the butler. "I came away with that upon my heart, that I could have wept too."

But now the ten minutes drew to an end. Poole disinterred the axe from under a stack of packing straw; the candle was set upon the nearest table to light them to the attack; and they drew near with bated breath to where that patient foot was still going up and down, up and down, in the quiet of the night.

"Jekyll," cried Utterson, with a loud voice, "I demand to see you." He paused a moment, but there came no reply. "I give you fair warning, our suspicions are aroused, and I must and shall see you," he resumed; "if not by fair means, then by foul! if not of your consent, then by brute force!

"Utterson," said the voice, "for God's sake, have mercy!"

Q 2) How does Stevenson make this such a tense and dramatic moment in the novel?

A 2) This is a very tense and dramatic moment in the novel due to the description of setting and events, which force the reader to feel suspense and to wonder whatever will happen next. The gothic setting and the vivid depiction of the characters add to the mystery and suspense in this passage.

Firstly, the detailed description of the gothic setting in this passage makes this moment very dramatic, as it forewarns something dark and otherworldly is going to happen:

"scud had banked over the moon, it was now quite dark... tossed the light of the candle to and fro...silently to wait".

This moment is very dramatic due to the heavy use of gothic weather. The 'scud' is described to cover the 'moon', which suggests that darkness is enveloping the house, which has gothic connotations of evil. The use of light imagery is furthered when the 'light' of the 'candle' is now the only source of light in the setting, which represents the fragility of the goodness in the world. The decrease in light also symbolises the decrease in knowledge on the case of Mr. Hyde. There is much more confusion, and the reader knows less which adds to the tension of the moment. The confusion is emulated as the setting is now 'quite dark' and Utterson is oblivious to what will greet him inside the door, which greatly increases the tension in the passage. The reader will simply have 'to wait' to find out. This use of light imagery to represent the positive attributes to the human soul and the Victorian Gentlemen ideal, as well as its superficiality and fragility due to the darkness enveloping it, is used throughout the novel, especially earlier on, when the 'shafts' of moonlight are only there for a brief moment and enlighten the desolate streets of London for a fleeting few seconds. That represents how little the characters realise the dangers of splitting apart the Victorian Gentlemen ideals and the bestial needs within.

Additionally, the vivid description of the restlessness of the characters adds tension to the passage as the reader finds this moment unnerving as well:

"the footman…very white and nervous…whispered Poole…conscious of a sudden chill of horror"

The anxiety of the characters in the passage makes the reader feel the same. This represents the Victorian society's complete inability to comprehend anything that is supernatural or which doesn't conform to their narrow-minded views and ideals and their abject terror when meeting anything like it. The 'footman' is described as 'white' and 'nervous' which symbolises his agitation at the thought of confronting some unexplained abnormality. His 'white' skin also represents his purity which is a stark contrast to the troglodytic monstrosity hiding behind the door. This ediginess is enhanced when Poole 'whisper[s]' to Utterson, not daring to speak aloud. His confusion represents Victorian society where the unnatural has no part. His fear comes from him not knowing what is happening. Even Utterson, the 'austere' lawyer feels a 'chill of horror' due to the gothic nature of what is happening. This creates great tension in the reader as the reader also doesn't understand what is happening and is anxious about what will happen next. This aversion to anything abnormal in Victorian society is clearly seen in Lanyon, who, due to his religious views, abhors the idea of changing or splitting oneself, and doesn't believe that the Victorian gentlemen have anything in common with the primordial rabble that lurk in the poorer parts of Victorian London. Due to his stubbornness, he died from shock when the truth was unveiled to him. Knowing this beforehand, the reader would feel very tense because they realise that something gothic and supernatural is going to happen.

Furthermore, the depiction of Hyde and his pathetic, animalistic characteristics adds tension to the passage as it represents the vulnerable side to the human soul:

"once I heard it weeping…for God's sake have mercy"

This moment is very dramatic as the reader finally understands what is behind the door. Its weakness and Utterson's stubbornness at not trying to understand, makes this very tense. The reader almost sympathises with Hyde due to his vulnerability. Hyde was said to have 'we[pt]', which shows us that he is in a state of shock and panic. But due to Victorian views, there is no 'mercy' for him and Utterson doesn't listen, causing him to commit suicide, which is very tense for the reader. The cruelty is amplified when Hyde pleads for 'mercy', likening him to an innocent, wounded animal. It is slightly ironic as he is asking for 'God's…mercy' but it is due to the religious views of Victorian society that there is no compromise with this unnatural creature, which also creates sympathy from the reader. This non-tolerance of unholy creatures is seen earlier in the play where everyone describes him as having some 'unknown deformity' and he has no place in the 'perfect', superficial society of Victorian England.

EXTRACT FOR Q3

"Did you ever remark that door?" he asked; and when his companion had replied in the affirmative, "It is connected in my mind," added he, "with a very odd story."

"Indeed?" said Mr. Utterson, with a slight change of voice, "and what was that?"

"Well, it was this way," returned Mr. Enfield: "I was coming home from some place at the end of the world, about three o'clock of a black winter morning, and my way lay through a part of town where there was literally nothing to be seen but lamps. Street after street, and all the folks asleep—street after street, all lighted up as if for a procession and all as empty as a church—till at last I got into that state of mind when a man listens and listens and begins to long for the sight of a policeman. All at once, I saw two figures: one a little man who was stumping along eastward at a good walk, and the other a girl of maybe eight or ten who was running as hard as she was able down a cross street. Well, sir, the two ran into one another naturally enough at the corner; and then came the horrible part of the thing; for the man trampled calmly over the child's body and left her screaming on the ground. It sounds nothing to hear, but it was hellish to see. It wasn't like a man; it was like some damned Juggernaut. I gave a view-halloa, took to my heels, collared my gentleman, and brought him back to where there was already quite a group about the screaming child. He was perfectly cool and made no resistance, but gave me one look, so ugly that it brought out the sweat on me like running. The people who had turned out were the girl's own family; and pretty soon, the doctor, for whom she had been sent, put in his appearance. Well, the child was not much the worse, more frightened, according to the Sawbones; and there you might have supposed would be an end to it. But there was one curious circumstance. I had taken a loathing to my gentleman at first sight. So had the child's family, which was only natural. But the doctor's case was what struck me. He was the usual cut-and-dry apothecary, of no particular age and colour, with a strong Edinburgh accent, and about as emotional as a bagpipe. Well, sir, he was like the rest of us; every time he looked at my prisoner, I saw that Sawbones turn sick and white with the desire to kill him. I knew what was in his mind, just as he knew what was in mine; and killing being out of the question, we did the next best. We told the man we could and would make such a scandal out of this, as should make his name stink from one end of London to the other. If he had any friends or any credit, we undertook that he should lose them. And all the time, as we were pitching it in red hot, we were keeping the women off him as best we could, for they were as wild as harpies. I never saw a circle of such hateful faces; and there was the man in the middle, with a kind of black, sneering coolness—frightened too, I could see that— but carrying it off, sir, really like Satan.

Q3) How does this moment in the novel imply to the reader the evil nature of Mr. Hyde?

A3) This moment in the novel strongly implies to the reader, the dark, pure evil nature of Mr. Hyde. We are presented a scene in which he injures an innocent child, which is enhanced through vivid imagery and description.

Firstly, the depiction of the gothic weather in the passage conveys that something bad is going to happen and it prolongs the wait and builds up the suspense and dread of the crime, which augments its evil nature:

"3 o'clock of a black winter morning…empty as a church…long for the sight of a policeman…"

The use of a '3 o'clock' time could refer to the 'demon hour' where evil is at its most powerful. This could be premonition of a supernatural, evil event about to occur. Also, a 'black winter morning' is a use of pathetic fallacy, and it uses light imagery, or the lack of it, to represent the hopelessness of the situation and how something malicious is about to happen. The simile, describing the setting as 'empty as a church' is a continuation of the religious theme. This shows that the faith in God has diminished and the devil is growing stronger and evil beings, like Hyde with the 'Devil's signature' on his 'face' are going to attack. It can also be interpreted as part of the theme science vs. religion and this people, like Lanyon, have lost their 'faith' in God, from seeing a troglodytic monster like Hyde. This heightens Hyde's malevolent nature as he is portrayed as powerful enough to destroy religious and Victorian 'made in God's own image' beliefs. Finally, the 'long[ing] for the sight of the policeman, suggests that some heinous crime is about to happen, and a policeman's presence would provide some comfort in the situation. The fact that all this malevolence is shown through different interpretations before Hyde is even seen, strengthens our perception of his pure, evil nature.

Furthermore, the description of the attack itself is very merciless and horrific, and this makes the attacker, Mr. Hyde, seem extremely wicked:

"trampled calmly over the child's body… left her screaming on the ground…it was hellish to see…like some damned juggernaut"

Hyde is described to have 'calmly' 'trampled' a 'child'. This is very horrific is it shows that he has no remorse over the fact that he hurt an innocent child. The use of 'body' almost makes it seem like she is already dead, and he is defiling her broken 'body'. His merciless nature is further seen when the child is depicted as 'screaming on the ground'. This evokes sympathy from the reader for the child and hate for Mr. Hyde. This imagery is shocking and it causes the reader to realise how evil Hyde is. Describing the attack as 'hellish' further enhances Hyde's satanic descriptions and how he is the embodiment of the Devil, from a religious point of view. This would have been especially traumatic for the Victorian reader as they were particularly religious. This biblical description is continued when he is described as a 'damned juggernaut'. This implies that even God has forsaken this creature and he is an unstoppable force of evil that no-one can restrain. This attack can also be a premonition of Carew's death, where he also is brutally attacked, but this time murdered as well, by the evil Hyde.

Additionally, the effect of Hyde's presence on other people, such as Enfield, is seen as very powerful and influential, and causes innocent people to think in warped, unjustified ways which shows the potency of his evil nature:

"turned sick and white with the desire to kill him…circle of such hateful faces…wild as harpies…like Satan"

The doctor is described to have turned 'sick and white' and wanted to 'kill' Hyde. A doctor is usually a caring figure, wanting to help people so this juxtaposition of doctor and 'kill' conveys to us how influential and addictive Hyde's evilness is. Portraying him as 'sick' could further the idea of Hyde's inner 'id' infecting other people. The use of the first person narrative really helps here as we can see Enfield's mind becoming warped every second, starting from describing them as a 'family' which later turned into a 'circle' of 'hateful faces. This could be a reference to the seven circles of hell. It could also symbolise how the evilness is surrounding the good and is overcoming them. The use of biblical monsters is furthered when he describes the women as 'wild as harpies' which could represent how strong Hyde's evil nature is to be able to turn other, innocent human beings into a tainted monstrosity, 'like Satan'.

Printed in Great Britain
by Amazon